This Won't
HURT
a Bit!

And Other Fractured Truths
in Healthcare

Especially For:

_____

This Won't HURT a Bit!
And Other Fractured Truths in Healthcare

Published by:
LaMoine Press
63 Pioneer, Suite 200
Hannibal, MO 63401
573-221-9086

Excerpts from the Journal of Nursing Jocularity reprinted with permission.

Cartoons on pages 7, 37, 45, 67 property of John Wise
Cartoons on pages 8, 15, 25, 57, 75, 85, and cover property of Bob Zahn

This Won't Hurt a Bit! is available at a special discount when purchased in bulk for special premiums, sales promotions, fundraising and educational needs. Special books may also be created to fit specific needs. Contact the Special Sales Director at LaMoine Press.

Cover and inside layout by Ad Graphics, Tulsa, OK • 918-252-1103
Photos by VIP Graphics, St. Louis, MO • 314-535-1117

All rights reserved (including the right to remain silent).

Printed in the Good Old USA

ISBN 0-9672090-0-5

This Won't HURT a Bit!

And Other Fractured Truths in Healthcare

Karyn Buxman, RN, MSN, CSP

LaMoine Press

"The first step in finding the humor in a situation is to assume that it's there."

- Karyn Buxman

Dedication

To Mom and Dad who
introduced me to the *lighter side* of
healthcare when I was still just a babe
(Marcus Welby—eat your heart out . . .).
And to Stan, David and Adam. Your
support, encouragement, patience, and
humor are what feeds me.

"A rubber chicken a day keeps the doctor away."

- Karyn Buxman

In Memory of Doug

"YES, IM A HYPOCHONDIAC, BUT IM A <u>SICK</u> HYPOCHONDRIAC!"

Contents

"Laughter is God's
hand wiping the tears
away from one's heart."

- *Karyn Buxman*

Foreword

I'm delighted that you are taking time to lighten up with this book. I believe firmly that laughter helps the medicine go down. *This Won't Hurt a Bit!* is a result of the many stories and jokes collected over numerous years from folks on the giving and receiving end of healthcare. Some were passed on by word-of-mouth, some were sent in letters, many were received via e-mail, and many were courtesy of the humor magazine designed specifically for nurses, *The Journal of Nursing Jocularity (JNJ)*.

With the untimely death of *JNJ* Publisher, Doug Fletcher, in 1998, we lost a valuable vehicle to communicate the lighter side of healthcare. And there's a lot of funny stuff out there. True, much of it is dark and twisted. The closer you are to tragedy and death, the darker your humor becomes. But humor gives us hope. It gives us relief. And it gives us victory.

This book doesn't have to be read in any particular order. Sit down, thumb through it, see what catches your fancy. And if you have a joke or story to share, please know that I'm anxious to hear it! *

Karyn Buxman, RN, MSN, CSP
Founder of HUMORx™

*Send them to:

HUMORx

P.O. Box 1273

Hannibal, MO 63401-1273

FAX: 573-221-7226

E-mail: Karyn@humorx.com

Acknowledgments

S pace does not allow me to list all who were influential in this final product. However, I simply must attempt to recognize those who were vital instruments in pulling this together. My National Speakers Association (NSA) buddies have been nudging (shoving) me to complete this project, especially Carol, Sam, Steve, Lois, Tony, Linda, Jeffrey, Kathy and my other dear friends who keep me in stitches (you know who you are). My nurse pals with humor vision, especially Patty, Melodie, Fran, John, Bob, Leslie and of course Doug, Georgia, Bob and Diane (I feel your spirit of humor with me every day). Kevin at VIP Graphics and Jim at Ad Graphics—you're terrific. Thanks to John Wise and Bob Zahn for your great cartoons. Wild Sal, I adore you! Amber and Bette, who somehow manage to keep some semblance of sanity in the office, no matter what my schedule, you guys are the best! And most especially, a huge thank you to all who have shared their stories.

Why did the rubber chicken cross the road? To get to the lighter side.

- *Karyn Buxman*

"CONGRATULATIONS, DEAR, YOU'RE THE SICKEST LOOKING ONE ON THE WHOLE FLOOR!"

"When tragedy and death cloud our lives, they darken our humor, as well."

- *Karyn Buxman*

Never a Dull Moment

Several years ago while working in a one room ICU, we had an unusual night when all the patients were sleeping. We decided to get some practice time with the resuscitation manikin, Resusci-Annie. We hauled her up from the practice lab in her suitcase, unpacked her and laid her in an empty bed. We all took turns giving her CPR. When we finished, we packed her in the suitcase and returned her to the practice lab. The next morning, the lady in the bed across from where we'd practiced motioned her doctor close and whispered, "Get me out of here! Last night the lady in that bed died and when they couldn't revive her they packed her in a suitcase!"   - *Andrea*

A weeping young man was led through the doors of the Emergency Department. He had fallen while in-line skating, lacerated his head and needed stitches. He was overcome with needle-phobia. He tried to be stoic, but soon became irrational with panic. He was so scared he shrieked, "Help me! Help me! Call 911! Where is William Shatner when you need him?!
- *Paula*

On our busy medical-surgical unit, there was an elderly man who would sit in his room and yell out continuously for no particular reason. His nurse thought she could calm him down by wheeling him over to the nurses' station where he could be around more people. When he started yelling again, she gently told him she didn't want to hear another peep out of him. After a few quiet moments, the patient looked over at his nurse with a grin on his face and said, "Peep!"   *- Judy*

We admitted a five-year-old boy into our last vacant bed— the room farthest from the nurses' station. Throughout the evening he played havoc with the staff by frequently pushing his call button. During shift change at 10:45 P.M. he called again. The oncoming nurse used the intercom and said, "What do you want, little boy?"

A long pause followed, then we heard his quivering voice respond, "Nothing, Wall." The child didn't ring the bell the rest of the night.   *- June*

A patient's wife passed by the nurses' station carrying a large, heavy cardboard box. A few moments later, the patient's call light went on. When the nurse entered the room, the patient asked if the nurse would give the box to his doctor.

The nurse peered into the box filled with phonograph records. "What's in the box?" asked the nurse.

The patient explained, "The doctor said to have my wife bring in all my old records."   *- Phyllis*

Years ago when I was a new grad, I worked on a med-surg floor. On one occasion I had a confused patient recovering from hip surgery. She was restrained with a posey vest and frequently screamed— loudly.

One evening, after listening to her for several hours, I tried all I knew to quiet her down. I gave up. I walked into her room, sat at her bedside and looked her right in the eyes.

"Honey," I said, "Stop screaming. You're driving me to drink."

She stopped screaming, patted me on the head and said, "Oh, sweetheart, don't blame me for your drinking problem."   - *Tracey*

Following a reprimand one evening, my three-year-old sat pouting in her highchair and said, "Mommy, I need to go to the doctor."

"Why honey?" I asked, thinking that something was wrong.

"Because," she replied sadly, "my feelings are hurting me."   - *Denise*

A patient rang his call light. The nurse answered through the intercom, "May I help you?"

"Can you come down here?"

"I'll be there in a minute."

"Is that a real minute or a nurse's minute?"   - *Angie*

Hopefully, they were playing a hand of poker, waiting for the anesthesia to take effect, but the last thing I remember before my operation began was my surgeon saying, "All right, who can open?" - K.L.

My father had a stroke and I stayed with him in the hospital, but after three days I was desperate to leave for a shower. The nurses were very busy, and I wanted my dad to be able to use the call button before I left. I demonstrated its use several times explaining, "This is how you call the nurse."

Before leaving I wanted to be sure he could summon help if necessary, so I asked him, "How do you get a nurse?"

He answered softly, "You tell her you love her."
- Simma

One of the nicest and most sincere cards I got when hospitalized was one that simply said, "Get Well Quick." It was from Blue Cross Blue Shield.

When assessing a patient, I asked him how long he had his cough. He replied, "I don't know. I've been out of town." - Cherry

I work in a busy office where a computer going down causes quite an inconvenience. Recently one of our computers not only crashed, it made a noise that sounded like a heart monitor. "This computer has flat-lined!" a co-worker called out with mock horror. "Does anyone here know how to do mouse-to-mouse?"

A s a pre-med student, I had to take a difficult class in physics. One day our professor was discussing a particularly complicated concept when a student rudely interrupted to ask, "Why do we have to learn this stuff?"

"To save lives," the professor responded quickly and continued the lecture.

A few minutes later, the same student spoke up again. "So how does physics save lives?" he persisted.

The professor replied, "It usually keeps the idiots like you out of medical school."

D uring a recent fire drill, I was closing doors to patients' rooms. An 86-year-old patient was talking on the phone when I reached her room. As I started to shut her door, she asked, "What's that ringing noise?"

"Don't worry," I said. "We're just having a little fire drill."

As I was leaving, I heard her say, "No, everything's just fine, dear. The hospital's on fire but a nice little nurse just came to lock me in my room."   - *Kathryn*

A s a new grad, I was a little nervous being in charge on the evening shift in the ER. My pulse quickened as an older man came in complaining of tightness in his chest and difficulty swallowing. I took his vital signs, determined he was not yet having difficulty breathing, and then called the physician to give him the patient's report. "How long has the man had this difficulty?" the doctor asked.

Unsure, I repeated the question to the patient. My stomach dropped when he replied, "Oh, since about 1947."   - Karyn

There was an elderly little lady in the room at the end of the hall of a med-surg unit. During the night, she kept climbing out of bed over the side rails and landing on the floor. After the third fall of the night, the patient was lying on the floor when the nurse rushed in.

She looked the nurse directly in the eye and said, "I just don't know how much more of this I can take!"
                                                        - Debra

During a recent change-of-shift report, I heard an IV infusion pump alarm. I asked one of our nurse's aides to go into the room and press the 'pause' button to stop the alarm. Our infusion pumps flash a message describing the problem, like 'air in the line'. When the aide returned to the nurses' station, I asked her what the pump was saying.

In earnest, she replied, "It was saying 'beep, beep, beep.'"   - Peggy

When a patient from a nursing home came to our emergency department with pneumonia, I contacted the next-of-kin listed on the patient's chart. After a fairly lengthy explanation of the serious nature of the patient's condition, I asked the family member, "So, are you the closest relative?"

She replied, "Oh no, honey! I live clear in Pennsylvania!"
— *Robin*

As a staff nurse on a busy neurological unit, I would go on morning rounds with the resident. Each person's level of orientation was assessed with questions like 'What day is it?', 'What month is it?' and 'Where are you?'.

Later in the day, I was making the bed in one of the patient's rooms. We had a casual conversation as the gentleman watched me work. As I put the pillow into the pillow case, he blurted out, "You can't do it that way!"

Startled, I asked him to tell me what I was doing wrong.

He said, "You have to put the pillow case on so I can read the hospital name printed on the end. Every day the doctors come in and ask me where I am and I read it off the pillow case."
— *Katie*

Overheard from another room, where there was a seven-year-old boy receiving his medicine from a nurse: "Johnny, we prefer to call this 'medication' rather than a 'fix.'"

A volunteer at a local hospital who sang songs and told jokes to entertain patients was leaving one day when he said to a patient, "I hope you get better."

The patient grumbled, "I hope you get better, too."
— *Dorothy*

A telephone repairman was working late in a large medical center and became lost. After a long search of the rambling first floor to find an exit, he spotted an elderly woman dressed in a volunteer uniform standing at the end of a corridor. "How do I get outside?" he asked her.

She smiled politely and said, "Dial 9."

A pediatric nurse was trying to calm her patient. "I wouldn't cry like that," she said.

The child sobbed and said, "It's the only way I know how."

After eight long months, a five-year-old boy finally got the call to come in for his kidney transplant. When the transplant coordinator went in to visit the boy and his parents, he was crying his eyes out, but wouldn't tell his parents why. Finally the coordinator sent the parents from the room so she could visit with him alone. When he could finally speak without crying, he said, "Is this kidney coming from a boy or a girl?"

"What difference would that make?" she asked encouragingly.

"Because. . . I don't want to have to sit down to pee!"
- *Lynnda*

One evening, I was assigned as the charge nurse on a medical-surgical floor. At the end of the hall were two women who had both suffered from strokes. 98-year-old Ida and 92-year-old Hilda were both quite senile and carried on intermittent nonsensical

conversations with each other all day and all night. I was busy making rounds when I heard them both speaking. Ida was crying, worried about whether she would go to heaven or hell when she died. She was obviously upset, but as I entered the room Hilda said to her, "Now listen, dearie, it doesn't matter to me where I go. The way I see it, I've got friends in both places."
- Julie

In our final year of nurses' training, a representative of the Organ Transplant Team explained the importance of donating any and all organs, then handed out uniform donor cards for each of us to sign. My friend, Veronica, shot me a puzzled look, leaned toward me and whispered, "Why would anyone want to donate their uniform?!"
- Lynn

"MY UNDERWEAR WAS CLEAN, MOM, UNTIL THE ACCIDENT."

I had an OB/GYN appointment the last time I was on call. I had been paged endlessly the entire day. I put my clothes on the chair next to the exam table with my beeper on top. At the exact moment the doctor palpated my breast, the beeper went off. In frustration, I said, "It does that all the time and drives me crazy!"

The MD looked at me very seriously and asked, "How do you make your breast do that?!"   - *Vicky*

I had a patient in the ER a couple of months ago who was 102 years old. The lady was extremely sharp for her age and all the staff commented how great it was that she could live so long.

"Well," she said, "it's not hard to live to be 102 ... You go to bed at night, you get up in the morning, you go to bed at night, you get up in the morning, you go to bed at night, you get up in the morning, and the next thing you know ... it's a hundred years."   - *Jim*

A patient arrived in the ER unable to speak, and after assessing the situation, I posted the patient's complaint on the flow boards as "Unable to speak."

The ER doc walked up to me and asked, "What's up with this guy?"

"Well, he's unable to speak," I replied.

"Yeah, but why?"

"He didn't say."   - *Peter*

Ann, a home health nurse, met her new patient, Mr. Jones, a quiet man who had a gorgeous head of hair. His chemotherapy had the potential to cause hair loss, and Ann voiced her concern about how he might react if this were to happen. Mr. Jones just smiled and said he could handle it.

The next day, Ann returned for a follow-up visit. Mrs. Jones opened the door, looking quite upset. Mr. Jones sat in the living room, wearing a hat and scowling. "What's wrong?" asked Ann.

Mr. Jones growled, "You said I might lose hair but this is ridiculous!" He pulled off his hat— he was totally bald!

Ann gasped, then noticed Mr. Jones break into a grin. She looked at his wife, who was also smiling— and holding up his toupee!   - Cheryl

Several years ago I worked on a med-surg unit with a sweet elderly lady who wore bilateral hearing aids.

As I prepared her for surgery, she followed all instructions and joked when she misunderstood what was said to her. Finally, right before going down to the OR, I asked her to remove both of her hearing aids. She pleasantly complied.

As I placed them in their cases, she smiled and said, "That's it! I'm off the air!"   - Jo

My classmate and I were doing our clinical rotation in the operating room. During surgery, Dr. Smith complained to the circulating nurse that the keys in his pocket got caught between the table and his thigh. He asked Miss Jones to slip her hand between his scrubs and cover gown and remove the keys. Miss Jones complied and the surgeon's face soon turned bright red. He jumped back from the table and cried, "Miss Jones! Miss Jones! That's not my pocket!"

- Marcia

The post-op report on my new pediatric patient said his family was Cambodian and could not understand English. Before they got to the floor, I tried to find an interpreter, but none was available. I spoke loudly and slowly when I greeted the family, thinking this would bridge the communication barrier. They smiled and acknowledged my greeting with nods.

I explained how they could control the room's temperature by adjusting the thermostat up or down. Wondering how I could ever make the family understand this complicated process, I turned and spoke very slowly and loudly, "Do you understand?"

Mom smiled and nodded. Then Dad asked, "You think it will be okay to keep the temperature around 72 degrees?"

- Terrie

During evening care, a fellow student nurse was preparing a post-surgical patient for sleep. She applied some paste from his bedside stand to his toothbrush and brought it to him with a kidney basin and some fresh water for rinsing.

Soon after he started brushing, he let out a loud "Yuk!" that I could hear all the way in the next room. The

student had confused the patient's toothpaste with
his hemorrhoid cream.   *- Victoria*

The pediatric resident was playing Santa on the
ward when the little boy sitting on his knee
couldn't remember what he wanted for Christmas.
Santa prompted him, "I know . . . You want peace on
earth and good will amongst men."

The boy replied, "No. Actually, it had something to do
with a gun."   *- Marian*

An acquaintance of mine who is a physician told
this story about her four-year-old daughter. On
the way to preschool, the doctor had left her
stethoscope on the car seat, and her little girl picked
it up and began playing with it. "Be still, my heart,"
thought my friend. "My daughter wants to follow in
my footsteps!"

Then the child spoke into the instrument: "Welcome
to McDonald's. May I take your order?"

One day I asked my patient, "Well, Thelma, how's
the world treating you?"

Thelma answered soberly, "It's not treating me. I'm
paying my way!"   *- Dorothy*

While performing an eye exam on a patient, the
nurse placed the patient twenty feet from the
chart and instructed, "Cover your right eye with your

hand and read the smallest line you can see clearly." He read the 20/20 line perfectly.

"Now your left." Again, a flawless read.

"Now both," the nurse requested. There was complete silence. The patient couldn't even read the large E on the top line.

The nurse turned and discovered that the patient had done exactly as instructed; he was standing there with both his eyes covered!

T wo of our most highly regarded surgeons had been working together for hours on an extremely difficult bowel resection. Dr. M was watching intently from above while Dr. B prepared to fire the End-To-End Anastomosis clip applier from below. The entire room was silent, praying all would go well.

Dr. B took a deep breath and grasped the stapler. In a voice full of the confidence gained through the vast experience of many years of surgery he proclaimed, "All right, here we go . . . hmmmm . . . lefty loosie and righty tighty."   - Tammy

It Only Hurts
When I Laugh

Q. What license plate indicates a urologist?

A. 2 P C ME

An elderly woman brought a butterfly mounted under glass when she had a doctor's appointment. The receptionist studied it for a moment and then said to her, "It's very pretty, Mrs. Smith, but it's not the specimen we had in mind."

Patient: "Doc, you gotta help me. I'm always forgetting stuff. What do I do?"

Doctor: "Pay me in advance."

A doctor, taking a history on his elderly patient, asked, "How old are you?"

"Ninety," said the man.

"Did you have a happy childhood?"

"So far, so good."

"I have a new hearing aid."
"What kind is it?"
"One o'clock."

Three elderly men went to the doctor for a memory test. The doctor said to the first man, "What is three times three?"

"274," he replied.

The doctor said to the second man, "It's your turn. What is three times three?"

"Tuesday," replied the second man.

The doctor said to the third man, "Okay, your turn. What's three times three?"

"Nine," said the third man.

"That's great!" said the doctor. "How did you get that?"

"Simple," said the third man. "I subtracted 274 from Tuesday."

A minister went to visit one of his elderly parishioners while she was sick in the hospital. She was napping so peacefully that he decided to sit at her bedside and wait until she woke up. While waiting, he saw a dish of peanuts next to her bedside and helped himself to a couple. A little later he helped himself to a few more. And before he knew it, he had eaten the entire dish. When she finally awoke, he apologized profusely, "Mabel, your peanut dish is empty. I promise to bring you some more when I come back to see you tomorrow."

"Oh, don't bother," she replied. "I can't eat them anyway. I just put them in that dish after I've sucked all the chocolate off of them!"

Q. What's the difference between God and a doctor?

A. God knows he's not a doctor.

A young woman went into a family planning clinic to ask how to prevent pregnancy. "A glass of cold water," answered the nurse.

"Before, during, or after?" asked the young woman.

"Instead."

Doctor: "Did you tell your husband you need a cholecystectomy?"

Patient: "Yes, but he says if he can't spell it, he can't afford it."

Secretary: "Doctor, the Invisible Man is waiting in the lobby for you."

Doctor: "Tell him I can't see him."

The obstetrician examined the patient and told her, "You have an ovarian fissure. If you deliver, it will be a miracle."

At home, her husband asked for a report. She hesitated. "I'm not sure. I think he said I have a fish, and if I deliver, it will be a mackerel."

Q. Where do you take a sick boat?

A. To a dock.

Q. Why do doctors dress so poorly?

A. Pharmaceutical reps don't give away clothing.

Q. Why do nurses like PMS?

A. Because once a month, they get to act like doctors.

"The doctor gave me two weeks to live."
"Goodness, what did you say?"
"I told him I'll take the first two weeks in May."

A couple of surgeons are out for drinks, boasting about their best work ever. The first one shares, "Last year my mother lost her eyesight completely in an accident. There was really no way to make her see again. Her eyeballs were completely ruined, so I took a chance and replaced her eyes with glass-eyes. I hooked them up with her nerves, and, what-do-you-know, today she sees perfectly!"

The other doctor nods, takes a sip of his drink then says, "A few months ago my uncle, who's a lumberjack, accidentally chopped off his right hand. I operated immediately and, having no other choice, replaced his hand with a rubber glove filled with sawdust. I connected it to the arm and after a few weeks, what-do-you-know, he's using it just fine!"

"Wait a darn minute," blurts the first surgeon. "Who's ever seen something like *that* happen?'"

"Your mother with her glass eyes . . . "

Q. How many psychologists does it take to screw in a light bulb?

A. Ten. One to screw it in and nine to share the experience.

D octor: "How long have you had the problem of forgetfulness?"
Patient: "What problem?"

D octor: "The tests are back and I'm still not sure what's causing your liver problems, but it may be due to drinking."
Patient: "Why don't you get back to me when you're sober, then?"

Q. How many psychiatrists does it take to change a light bulb?

A. One, but the bulb must really *want* to change.

Q. How many chiropractors does it take to change a light bulb?

A. One . . . But it takes 15 visits and four x-rays.

Four doctors were out duck hunting, but it was hunting season for only one of the ducks in the region. After many hours on the boat without seeing a single duck, they dozed off. The general practitioner awoke to see a flock of ducks flying over. Unsure if the ducks were in season, he consulted the specialist.

The specialist wasn't sure, so he woke up the surgeon. As soon as the surgeon saw the ducks, he started blasting and hit half a dozen.

"Are you sure those were the ducks in season?" the first two doctors asked.

The surgeon replied, "Wake up the pathologist and ask him."

Q. What's the prognosis for a patient whose left side is removed?

A. The patient will be all right.

The ER nurse started to assess her patient. "How old are you?"

"I'm fifty."

"Your record says you're 52."

"I would have been, but I've been sick for two years."

Doctor: "Mr. Smith, that last check you gave me came back."

Patient: "Then we're even, Doctor. So did my arthritis."

Q. Why do patients wear blue elastic caps in the OR?

A. Because 'everything's better with blue bonnet on it.'

The mother was very excited when she called the doctor. "Doctor! Doctor!" she shouted. "My son just swallowed a bullet! What should I do?"

"Stay calm," advised the doctor. "Just give him some castor oil and make sure you don't aim him at anybody."

Q. What's the difference between a nun and a nurse?

A. A nun only has to serve one god.

Q. How many pre-med students does it take to change a light bulb?

A. Five. One to change the bulb and four to pull the ladder out from under him.

Q. If a tonsillectomy is the removal of your tonsils, an appendectomy is the removal of your appendix and a splenectomy is the removal of your spleen, what is the removal of a growth from your head?

A. A haircut.

Q. What did the Dentist of the Year get?

A. A little plaque.

A wife became concerned about her overworked husband and took him to their physician for a checkup. The office nurse led them to the exam room and took the husband's vital signs. She then took the wife aside and whispered, "I don't like the way your husband looks."

"I don't either," replied the wife, "but he's a good father to the children."

Q. What's the difference between a surgeon and a puppy?

A. Eventually the puppy grows up and quits whining.

Three health care professionals find themselves at the Pearly Gates. Saint Peter asks the first, "Why do you belong here?"

The first replies, "I was a great surgeon. I have saved countless lives."

"Welcome," says Saint Peter, "We've been expecting you."

Saint Peter then asks the second, "Why do you belong here?"

The second answers, "I was a family practitioner. I treated young and old alike. I made them well again."

"Welcome," says Saint Peter, "We've been expecting you."

Finally, Saint Peter asks the third, "Why do you belong here?"

The third says, "I ran an HMO. I helped allow for thousands to receive medical care."

"Okay, come in," replies Saint Peter, "but you can only stay a day and a half."

A man was brought to Mercy Hospital and taken quickly in for heart surgery. The operation went well and as the groggy man regained consciousness, he was reassured by a Sister of Mercy, who was waiting by his bed.

"Mr. Smith, you're going to be just fine," said the nun, gently patting his hand. "We do need to know, however, how you intend to pay for your stay here. Are you covered by insurance?"

"No, I'm not," the man whispered hoarsely.

"Can you pay in cash?" persisted the nun.

"I'm afraid I can't, Sister."

"Well, do you have any close relatives?" asked the nun.

"Just my sister in New Mexico," he volunteered. "But she's a humble spinster nun."

"Oh, I must correct you, Mr. Smith. Nuns are not 'spinsters'. They are married to God."

"Wonderful," said Smith. "In that case, please send the bill to my brother-in-law."

A lady came to the hospital to visit a friend. She hadn't been in a hospital for several years and felt very ignorant about the new technologies. A technician followed her onto the elevator, wheeling a large machine with tubes and wires and dials and lights. She studied it for a moment and then said, "Boy, I would hate to be hooked up to that thing."

"So would I," replied the technician. "It's a floor cleaning machine."

Bernice's husband had been slipping in and out of a coma for several months, yet she stayed by his bedside every single day. When he came to, he motioned for her to move closer, then whispered hoarsely, "I've realized something... You have been with me all through the bad times. When I got fired, you were by my side. When my business fell, you were there. When I got shot, you were with me. When we lost the house, you gave me support. When my health started failing, you were still by my side.

"When I think about it now, Bernice, I think you bring me bad luck."

A t a pharmacy, Stella asked to use the infant scale to weigh the baby she held in her arms. The clerk explained that the device was out for repairs, but said that she could figure the infant's weight by weighing Stella and the baby together on the adult scale, then weighing the mother alone and subtracting the second amount from the first.

"It won't work," Stella countered. "I'm not the mother. I'm the aunt."

A fter living to a ripe old age, Dr. Jones, a world-famous surgeon, passed away during his sleep. He found himself at the back of an extremely long line leading to the Pearly Gates.

After waiting what seemed like an eternity, Dr. Jones decided that he shouldn't have to wait in line. He walked up to the Pearly Gates and said to St. Peter, "I'm Dr. Benny Jones, world famous surgeon. While on earth, I saved many lives and cured countless illnesses. I don't think I should have to wait in this line."

St. Peter curtly replied, "Here in Heaven, everyone is treated the same. Now go back to the end of the line."

As he walked to the back of the line, he noticed a gentleman in a white lab coat with a leather bag and stethoscope, obviously a doctor, walk up to the front of the line. St. Peter waved him right through.

Furious, Dr. Jones ran up to St. Peter and shouted, "Why did that doctor get to go right through?"

St. Peter smiled and said, "Oh, that was God. Sometimes he just likes to play doctor."

Patient: "This hospital is no good. They treat us like dogs."

Nurse: "Mr. Martin, you know that's not true. Now roll over."

A patient was in his psychiatrist's office for his first appointment. "What seems to be the problem?" asked the physician.

"I'm a wig wam ... I'm a tee-pee ... I'm a wig wam ... I'm a tee pee ... I'm a wig wam ... I'm a tee-pee ..." the patient kept repeating.

The doctor thought for a moment, and then replied, "Your problem is obvious. You're two tents."

Q. How can you tell if you have a cheap doctor?

A. He takes Friday off to play miniature golf.

A couple of nurses went to the Halloween party in unusual costumes: He had on an army shirt and helmet; she wore army pants and combat boots. They went as upper and lower GIs.

Mabel, who is 63 years old, goes to her doctor for her annual physical. He examines her thoroughly and said, "Mabel, I've got good news and bad news for you."

Mabel said, "What's the good news?" The doctor said, "You are in wonderful shape. I can't find anything at all wrong with you."

Mabel then asked, "What's the bad news?"

The doctor said, "You're pregnant."

Mabel flew out of his office. She was very upset, and ran home and called her husband at work. When he answered, she said, "You old goat! You got me pregnant!"

After a long pause he said, "Who's calling?"

An accountant is having a hard time sleeping and goes to see his doctor.

"Doctor, I just can't get to sleep at night."

"Have you tried counting sheep?"

"That's the problem. I make a mistake and then spend three hours trying to find it."

A guy had been feeling down for so long that he finally decides to seek the aid of a psychiatrist. He lies on the couch, spills his guts, and then waits for the profound wisdom of the psychiatrist to make him feel better.

The psychiatrist sits in silence for a few minutes with a puzzled look on his face. Suddenly, he looks up with an expression of delight and says, "Um, I think your problem is low self-esteem. It's very common among losers."

A man was taking his wife, who was pregnant with twins, to the hospital when his car went out of control and crashed. Upon regaining consciousness, he saw his brother, a relentless world-class practical joker, sitting at his bed side.

He asked his brother how his wife was and his brother replied, "Don't worry, everybody is fine and you have a son and a daughter. But the hospital was in a real hurry to get the birth certificates filed and since both you and your wife were unconscious, I named them for you."

The husband was thinking to himself, "Oh no, what has he done now?" and said with trepidation, "Well, what did you name them?"

The brother replied, "I named the little girl Denise."

The husband, relieved, said, "That's a very pretty name! What did you come up with for my son?"

The brother replied, "Denephew."

Two interns were watching an elderly gentleman move slowly down the hall.

"I'll bet you $5 he's had a hemorrhoidectomy."

"No way. He's suffering from arthritis."

They both approached the man to inquire.

"Why are you moving so slowly, sir?" asked one intern.

The old man replied, "My slippers are too large."

A mother told the ER nurse, "My son swallowed an ink pen."

The nurse replied, "Okay, the doctor will be able to look at him in about ten minutes."

"What will I do until then?" asked the woman.

"Use a pencil."

The doctor exclaimed to the plumber, "Your fee is $150 an hour?! I only charge $100 an hour!"

The plumber replied, "Yeah, that's all I was making when I was a doctor."

A 92-year-old man went to the doctor to get a physical. A few days later the doctor saw the man walking down the street with a gorgeous young lady on his arm. A couple of days later the doctor talked to the man and said, "You're really doing great, aren't you?"

The man replied, "Just doing what you said, Doctor. 'Get a hot mamma and be cheerful.'"

The doctor said, "I didn't say that. I said you got a heart murmur. Be careful."

The new Medical Director of the hospital goes into his brand new office. He tries out his brand new desk, brand new chair, even his new pencils. A nurse knocks on the door so, wanting to impress her, he picks up the phone, tells her to come in and then begins talking on the phone:

"Yes, Mr. President, I'd be glad to give you some advice on the health care issue. Give the Senator my thanks for recommending me."

He hung up and turned to the nurse. "What do you want?"

"Nothing, Doctor. Just passing on the message from the workmen that they might be able to connect your telephone this afternoon."

"I think I've lived too long," complained the elderly patient.

"No," replied the doctor. "You've just lived past the fun part."

Q. What do insurance and a hospital gown have in common?

A. You just think you're covered.

Q. What happens when a heart specialist gets stopped by the highway patrol?

A. A cardiac arrest.

A recent bride accompanied her husband to the doctor's office. After the husband had a checkup, the doctor took the wife aside and said, "If you don't do the following, your husband will surely die:

"Each morning fix him a healthy, hearty breakfast including hand-squeezed orange juice and Belgian waffles. Send him off to work with a kiss on his cheek, a whisper of love, and a good mood.

"At lunch time make him a warm, nutritious meal, give him a back and shoulder massage and put him in a good frame of mind.

"For dinner, fix an especially nice meal accompanied by candlelight and music, and don't burden him with household chores.

"Make love to him passionately several times a week. Be tender with him, do whatever he asks you to do as if you were on another honeymoon, and satisfy his every whim."

Afterwards on the way home, the husband asked his wife what the doctor had to say.

She replied, "He said you're going to die."

Confucius say, "Patient who steps on invoice foots the bill."

Dentist: "How did you lose all your teeth at once?"
Man: "I left them on the washstand."

What can doctors do that no one else can?
Read their own writing.

The ophthalmologist was also a psychiatrist. During each examination he would ask, "What do you really see?"

Patient: "Doctor, I fell down and ache all over. But I don't want any x-rays, pills, shots, lab tests, or hospital stays."

Doctor: "What do you want then?!"

Patient: "You tell me— you're the doctor!"

Doctor: "To what do you attribute your longevity?"

Patient: "I was born in 1893."

Caller to Ask-A-Nurse: "She's flopping on the bed, turning colors and gasping for air. What do I do?"

Nurse: "Put her back in the aquarium immediately!"

"The doctor said I was suffering from depression. 'If it was me,' he said, 'I'd go home and take my wife out for dinner and a few drinks.'"

"So what are you going to do?"

"I'm picking up his wife at six thirty."

A nurse catches her physician in the hallway at the hospital and says, "Doctor, I need you to help me. Every time I go to the bathroom, dimes come out!" The doctor tells her to relax, go home, rest with her feet up and touch base with him in a week.

A week later the nurse returns to work, bumps into the doctor and says, "Doctor, it's gotten worse! Every time I go to the bathroom, quarters come out! What's wrong with me?" Again the doctor tells her to relax, go home, rest with her feet up and look him up in a week.

Another week passes and the nurse returns to work. She hunts the doctor down, grabs his arms and says, "Listen, doc, I'm still not getting better! Every time I go to the bathroom, half-dollars come out! WHAT THE HECK IS WRONG WITH ME?!"

The doctor says, "Relax, you're just going through the change!"

A 92-year-old woman had a full cardiac arrest at her home in the backwoods and was rushed to the hospital. After about thirty minutes of unsuccessful resuscitation attempts the old lady was pronounced dead. The doctor went to tell the lady's 78-year-old daughter that her mother didn't make it.

"Didn't make it? Where could they be? She left in the ambulance forty-five minutes ago!"

Nancy Nurse lived an exemplary life. She was devoted to her family, worked full time at the university medical center, taught CPR in the community on Tuesday nights, faithfully attended her church, gave generously to a host of charities, and had a kind word for everyone.

After the death of her husband and the mourning period had passed, her nursing supervisor said to her, "Nancy, you inherited a healthy amount from your husband. All your life you have done for others, and given yourself next to nothing. Now is your chance to have a good time, before you're too old to enjoy it!"

Nancy took these words to heart. She went to a plastic surgeon who made her look ten years younger. Then she had her hair cut, colored and permed, and purchased a stylish new wardrobe, designer sunglasses and a bright red Cadillac convertible.

Nancy was cruising down the road on the way to the airport, about to experience the trip she had always dreamed of but had never taken. Suddenly, a bolt of lightning flashed down, killing her instantly.

Standing before God, she asked respectfully, "Lord, how could you do this to me? I'm Nancy Nurse. I have carried out your Commandments, and have lived a righteous life. Now, just when I was about to enjoy a few pleasures, why did you see fit to strike me down?"

God looked at her closely. "I'm sorry, Nancy," He said. "I just didn't recognize you!"

Every night, a good old boy named Bubba goes to the store, buys six cans of beer and goes home to drink them in front of the TV. One night, after his sixth can, the doorbell rings. Bubba staggers out and opens the door. Outside on the porch is a 6-foot tall cockroach. Bubba is shocked when the cockroach elbows its way into the hall, grabs Bubba by the neck and throws him halfway up the stairs. When Bubba comes around, the cockroach is gone and he reckons the pain is from too much beer.

The next night, Bubba has just finished his fourth can of beer when the doorbell rings again. He weaves his way to the door and there outside is the 6-foot tall cockroach again. It punches him in the head, kicks him in the ankle and when Bubba regains consciousness, again— no cockroach.

The third night, after only two cans of beer, the doorbell rings. Bubba, practically sober, warily opens the door and the cockroach is there again. It hits him with a baseball bat, bites him on the arm and kicks both his kneecaps. Once more it vanishes.

Now worried, Bubba vows not to drink again and is shocked when the next night, utterly sober, he has the living daylights beaten out of him by this 6-foot tall cockroach on the doorstep.

Bubba goes to the doctor to explain what's been happening and the doctor listens. "Doctor," he moans, "What's the matter with me?"

"Don't worry," reassures the doctor. "There's just a nasty bug going around."

Two children were sitting outside a clinic. One of them was crying very loudly.

2nd Child: "Why are you crying?"

1st Child: "I came here for my blood test."

2nd Child: "So? Are you afraid?"

1st Child: "No, not that. For the blood test, they cut my finger."

At this, the second one started crying. Puzzled, the first one asked, "Why are you crying?"

2nd Child: "I've come for my urine test!"

"I'm prescribing these pills for you," the doctor told the retired husband who tipped the scales at more than two hundred fifty pounds.

"I don't want you to swallow them," he added ... "Just spill them on the floor twice a day and pick them up one at a time."

A psychiatrist was doing his normal morning rounds when he entered a patient's room. He found Lloyd sitting on the floor, pretending to saw a piece of wood in half. Floyd was hanging from the ceiling by his feet. The doctor asked Lloyd what he was doing. The patient replied, "Can't you see I'm sawing this piece of wood in half?"

The doctor inquired of Lloyd what Floyd was doing. Lloyd replied, "Oh, he's my friend, but he's a little crazy. He thinks he's a light bulb." The doctor looked up and noticed Floyd's face turning bright red.

The doctor told Lloyd, "If he's your friend, you should get him down from there before he hurts himself."

Lloyd replied, "What? And work in the dark?"

A man was terribly overweight so his doctor put him on a diet. "I want you to eat regularly for two days, then skip a day, and repeat this procedure for two weeks. The next time I see you, you'll have lost at least five pounds."

When the man returned, he shocked the doctor by losing nearly twenty pounds. "Why, that's amazing!" the doctor said. "Did you follow my instructions?"

The man nodded. "I'll tell you though, I thought I was going to drop dead that third day."

"From hunger, you mean?"

"No, from skipping."

A young man called the hospital and shouted at the nurse, "You gotta send help! My wife's going into labor!"

The nurse said, "Calm down. Is this her first child?"

"No!" he cried urgently. "This is her husband!"

Olympic Gold Medalist, Picabo (Peek-A-Boo) Street, through endorsements and other perks, amassed a tidy sum for a young lady. In her quest for sharing her good fortune with people in her community, and because she had spent so much time in the local hospital with multiple surgeries for knee injuries, Street donated a sizable amount of money to the hospital to be used at their discretion. In need of better facilities, the hospital put her donation to work in their Intensive Care Unit, now known as the Picabo I. C. U.

Ol' Bert had been a faithful Christian and was in the hospital, near death. The family called their pastor to be with them. As the pastor stood next to the bed, Ol' Bert's condition appeared to deteriorate and he motioned frantically for something to write on. The pastor lovingly handed him a pen and a piece of paper, and Ol' Bert used his last bit of energy to scribble a note, then he died.

As doctors and nurses rushed into the room, the pastor tucked the note in his pocket for safe keeping. At the funeral, as he was finishing the message, he realized that he was wearing the same jacket that he'd worn when Ol' Bert died. He said, "You know, Ol' Bert handed me a note just before he died. I haven't looked at it, but knowing Bert, I'm sure there's a word of inspiration there for us all."

He opened the note and read, "Hey Goofball, you're standing on my oxygen tube!"

Two little kids are in a hospital, lying on stretchers next to each other, outside the operating room. The first kid leans over and asks, "What are you in here for?"

The second kid says, "I'm in here to get my tonsils out and I'm a little nervous."

The first kid says, "You've got nothing to worry about. I had that done when I was four. They put you to sleep, and when you wake up they give you lots of Jell-O and ice cream. It's a breeze!"

The second kid then asks, "What are you here for?"

The first kid says, "A circumcision."

The second kid responds, "Whoa! I had that done when I was born. I couldn't walk for a year!"

"I SEE A LOT OF THAT... TV REMOTE CONTROL THUMB."

A nursing assistant, floor nurse, and charge nurse from a small nursing home were eating lunch in the break room. In walked a lady dressed in silk scarfs and wearing large polished stone jewelry.

"I am 'Gina the Great,'" exclaimed the lady. "I am so pleased with the way you have taken care of my aunt that I will now grant the next three wishes!"

The nurses argued among themselves as to who would ask for the first wish. Speaking up, the nursing assistant said, "I wish I were on a tropical island beach with single, well-built men feeding me fruit and tending to my every need." With a puff of smoke, the nursing assistant vanished.

The floor nurse said, "I wish I was rich and retired and spending my days in my own warm cabin at a ski resort with handsome guys feeding me cocoa and doughnuts." With a puff of smoke, she, too, was gone.

"Now, what is the last wish?" asked the lady. The charge nurse said, "I want those two back on the floor at the end of the lunch break."

A couple of women were playing golf one sunny Saturday morning. The first of the twosome teed off and watched in horror as her ball headed directly toward a foursome of men playing the next hole.

Indeed, the ball hit one of the men, and he immediately clasped his hands together between his legs, fell to the ground and proceeded to roll around in evident agony. The woman rushed down to the man and immediately began to apologize. She said, "Please allow me to help. I'm a physical therapist and I know I could relieve your pain if you'd allow."

"Ummph, ohhhhh, nooo, I'll be all right...I'll be fine in a few minutes," he replied breathlessly as he remained in the fetal position still clasping his hands together between his legs.

But she persisted, and he finally allowed her to help him. She gently took his hands away and laid them to the side, and began to massage his leg. She then asked him, "How does that feel?"

He cocked one eye and said, "It feels great, but my thumb still hurts like crazy."

When doctors were told to vote on a merger with another hospital:

The allergists voted to scratch it.

The dermatologists preferred no rash moves.

The gastroenterologists had a gut feeling about it.

The microsurgeons were thinking along the same vein.

The neurologists thought the administration had a lot of nerve.

The obstetricians stated they were laboring under a misconception.

The ophthalmologists considered the idea short-sighted.

The orthopedists issued a joint resolution.

The parasitologists said, "Well, if you encyst."

The pathologists yelled, "Over my dead body!"

The pediatricians said, "Grow up."

The proctologists said, "We are in arrears."

The psychiatrists thought it was madness.

The surgeons decided to wash their hands of the whole thing.

The radiologists could see right through it.

The internists thought it was a hard pill to swallow.

The plastic surgeons said, "This puts a whole new face on the matter."

The podiatrists thought it was a big step forward.

The D.O.s thought they were being manipulated.

The urologists felt the scheme wouldn't hold water.

The anesthesiologists thought the whole idea was a gas.

The cardiologists didn't have the heart to say no.

And the otologists were deaf to the idea.

The pending merger didn't fly!

A new nurse listened while the doctor was yelling, "Typhoid! Tetanus! Measles!"

The new nurse asked another nurse, "Why is he doing that?"

The other nurse replied, "Oh, he just likes to call the shots around here."

Dr. Weinstein was an obstetrician/gynecologist for 25 years. One day, he decided he just couldn't deliver one more baby. He was burned-out, so he decided to completely change professions and enrolled in an auto mechanics course to become an auto mechanic.

After several months he took his final exam and was totally surprised when he made a score of 200 on a test with a possible score of 100. He approached the instructor and asked how he got such a score.

The instructor explained, "Well, Dr. Weinstein, you correctly disassembled the engine for 50 points, and you correctly reassembled the engine for another 50 points and I gave you an extra 100 points for doing it all through the muffler!"

H MO receptionist: "The earliest appointment I can give you is in six weeks."

Patient: "I could be dead by then."

Receptionist: "No problem. The visit can always be canceled."

Q. Why do IV therapy nurses frequently experience burnout?

A. Because their best work is frequently in vein.

Q. How many nurses does it take to screw in a light bulb?

A. None. That's engineering's job.

Q. How many nurses with PMS does it take to change a light bulb?

A. None of your *&%$# business!

Q. How many nurses does it take to change a light bulb?

A. An impossible task— according to OSHA regulations, no one has been properly trained.

Q. How many nurses does it take to change a light bulb?

A. One. She figured out the light bulb was okay. The doctor forgot to turn the switch on.

Q. How many doctors does it take to change a light bulb?

A. It depends. How much insurance does the light bulb have?

Q. How many nurses does it take to change a light bulb?

A. Five. One to change the bulb, one to check the policy and procedure, one for documentation, one for quality assurance, and one for the Task Force on Hospital Lighting.

Q. How many gynecologists does it take to change a light bulb?

A. They don't bother. They say, "Why don't you let me take out the socket? You're not using it and it will only cause you trouble in the future."

Q. How many physical therapists does it take to change a light bulb?

A. Only one, but it requires a lot of adaptive equipment.

What Doctors Say, And *What They're Really Thinking*:

"This should be taken care of right away."

I'd planned a trip to Hawaii next month but this is so easy and profitable that I want to fix it before it cures itself.

"There is a lot of that going around."

My God, that's the third one this week. I'd better learn something about this.

"Well . . . what have we here . . . ?"

I have no idea— let's hope you can give me a clue.

"Let me check your medical history."

I want to see if you've paid your last bill before spending any more time with you.

"Why don't we make another appointment later in the week?"

I need the bucks, so I'm charging you for another office visit.

"We have some good news and some bad news."

The good news is, I'm going to buy that new BMW. The bad news is, you're going to pay for it.

"Let me schedule you for some tests."

I have a 40% interest in the lab.

"I'd like to have my associate look at you."

He's going through a messy divorce and owes me a bundle.

"If it doesn't clear up in a week, give me a call."

I don't know what it is. Maybe it will go away by itself.

"That's quite a nasty looking wound."

I think I'm going to throw up.

"This may smart a little."

Last week two patients bit off their tongues.

"Well, we're not feeling so well today, are we . . . ?"

I'm stalling for time. Who are you and why are you here?

The nurse will go over your diet instructions with you.

I can't begin to remember what you can eat on this diet.

"This should fix you up."

The drug company slipped me some big bucks to prescribe this stuff.

"Do you suppose all this stress could be affecting your nerves?"

You're crazier'n an outhouse rat. Now, if I can only find a shrink who'll split fees with me . . .

"If those symptoms persist, call for an appointment."

I've never heard of anything so disgusting. Thank God I'm off next week.

Two cardiac patients shared a room in the CCU. One night one of them arrested and resuscitation attempts failed. The room was cleaned and another patient was admitted in his place. After the nurse left, the new patient noticed his monitor and asked the roommate what it was. "I'm not sure what it's called. But if you break it, they beat you to death."

"My doctor said I'm a hypochondriac."
"How does that make you feel?"
"I'm just sick about it."

Nurse: "Why do you have a pocket full of teaspoons?"

Patient: "The doctor said to take one every four hours."

The husband watched intently as the nurse put the thermometer under his wife's tongue. After a moment of silence, he finally asked the nurse, "What do you charge for that instrument?"

After marrying a young woman, a ninety-year-old man told his doctor that they were expecting a baby. "Let me tell you a story," said the doctor. "An absent-minded fellow went hunting, but instead of a gun, he picked up an umbrella. Suddenly a bear charged at him. Pointing his umbrella at the bear, he shot and killed it on the spot."

"Impossible!" the geezer exclaimed. "Somebody else must have shot that bear."

"Exactly," replied the doctor.

Three buddies die in a car crash and they go to heaven for an orientation. They are all asked, "When you are in your casket and friends and family are mourning upon you, what would you like to hear them say about you?"

The first guy says, "I would like to hear them say that I was a great doctor of my time, and a great family man."

The second guy says, "I would like to hear that I was a wonderful husband and school teacher who made a huge difference in our children of tomorrow."

The last guy replies, "I would like to hear them say . . . LOOK, HE'S MOVING!"

Patient: "It's been one month since my last visit and I still feel miserable."

Doctor: "Did you follow the instructions on the medicine I gave you?"

Patient: "I sure did. The bottle said, 'Keep tightly closed.'"

A therapist suggested exercise might improve the man's sexual performance. "Try walking ten miles a day and call me in a week."

After a week, the patient called.

"Any improvement?" asked the therapist.

"I don't know. I'm seventy miles from home."

A funeral procession was going up a steep hill in San Francisco when the casket fell out of the hearse and began sliding down the hill. It forced cars and pedestrians to swerve out of its way as it slid and spun and bumped and jumped down the hill. It was going 90 m.p.h. when it reached the curb with a bang and the top flew open, propelling the body through the air and through the window of a doctor's office. It landed in a chair opposite the doctor, who was busy doing paperwork. The doctor looked up and asked, "Can I help you?"

"Can you give me something to stop this coffin?"

D octor: "I can't understand why Mr. Brown hasn't paid his bill yet."

Billing Clerk: "He called and said that his recovery was such a miracle, he sent the check to a church instead."

W ife to the psychotherapist: "Now I'll tell my husband's side of the story."

D octor: "How is the child who swallowed a dime?"
Nurse: "No change yet."

A man thought his dog died, but to verify it, he took the body to the vet. The vet put the dog on the table, got a cat and had the cat walk clockwise twice around the dog, then counterclockwise twice. The vet said, "I'm sorry. It looks like your dog is truly dead."

The man, stricken with grief, stopped by the clerk to pay his bill. "That will be $425," said the receptionist.

"$425! Why so much money?" the man demanded.

"It's $25 for the office visit and $400 for the cat scan."

N urse: "Did you hear about the man in 22B? Now that the transplant is over, he wants to go back to his wife."

Doctor: "Yeah, I guess he had a change of heart."

W hile making her rounds, the head nurse noticed a young female patient missing. Pressing the intercom, she asked, "Jenni, where's the patient in 340?"

"Oh!" came the reply. "Well . . . she was complaining of severe chills, so I put her in bed with Mr. Harper in 328 who was running a high fever."

A hillbilly was making his first visit to a hospital where his teenage son was about to have an operation. Watching the doctor's every move, he asked, "What's that fer?"

The doctor explained, "This is an anesthetic. After he gets this, he won't know a thing."

"Save your time, Doc," exclaimed the man. "He don't know nothing now."

Morris complained to his friend Irving that love making with his wife was becoming routine and boring.

"Get creative Morris. Break up the monotony. Why don't you try 'playing doctor' for an hour? That's what I do," said Irving.

"Sounds great," Morris replied, "but how do you make it last for an hour?"

"Just keep her in the waiting room for 55 minutes!"

A 60-year-old man went to a doctor for a checkup. The doctor told him, "You're in terrific shape. There's nothing wrong with you. Why, you might live forever; you have the body of a 35-year-old. By the way, how old was your father when he died?"

The 60-year-old responded, "Did I say he was dead?"

Surprised, the doctor asked, "How old is he and is he very active?"

The 60-year-old responded, "Well, he's 82 years old and he still goes skiing three times a season and surfing three times a week during the summer."

The doctor couldn't believe it, so he asked, "Well, how old was your grandfather when he died?"

The 60-year-old responded again, "Did I say he was dead?"

The doctor was astonished. He said, "You mean to tell me you are 60 years old and both your father and your grandfather are alive? Is your grandfather very active?"

The 60-year-old said, "He goes skiing at least once a season and surfing once a week during the summer. Not only that," said the patient, "my grandfather is 106 years old, and next week he's getting married again."

The doctor exclaimed, "A 106 years old! Why on earth would your grandfather want to get married?"

His patient looked up at the doctor and said, "Did I say he wanted to?"

A pre-med student is taking an examination and the last question is, "List four advantages of breast milk."

The student began to answer the question:

1. No need to sterilize bottles

2. Healthier for the child

3. Available whenever necessary

But the fourth point eluded him. When there was only a couple of minutes left to finish the exam he got desperate and answered:

4. Available in attractive containers

A woman took her 16-year-old daughter to the doctor. The doctor asked, "Okay, Mrs. Jones, what's the problem?"

The mother said, "It's my daughter, Darla. She keeps getting these cravings, she's putting on weight, and is sick most mornings."

The doctor gave Darla a thorough examination, then turned to the mother and said, "Well, I don't know how to tell you this, but your Darla is pregnant— about four months, would be my guess."

The mother cried out, "Pregnant? She can't be! She has never ever been left alone with a man, have you, Darla?"

Darla answered, "No mother. I've never even kissed a man!"

The doctor walked over to the window and just stared outside. About five minutes passed and finally the mother asked, "Is there something wrong out there, Doctor?"

The doctor replied, "No, not really. It's just that the last time anything like this happened, a star appeared in the east and three wise men came over the hill. I'll be darned if I'm going to miss it this time!"

The doctor sent her patient a bill for a physical. The patient didn't pay even though the doctor resubmitted the bill four times. Finally, the doctor sent a picture of her infant daughter with a note saying, "The reason I need the money."

A week later the patient responded— no check, but a picture of a gorgeous woman with a mink coat, and written on the back of the picture, "The reason I can't pay."

Q. What is a waiting room?

A. A place where a person becomes patient.

Q. What do you get when you cross an elephant and a skin doctor?

A. A pachydermatologist.

Q. What is a common ailment for roofers?

A. Shingles.

Q. What do you get when you mix Milk of Magnesia and vodka?

A. A Phillips Screwdriver.

Nurse taking a patient's history: "When is your birthday?"

Patient: "June 10th."

Nurse: "What year?"

Patient: "Every year."

Patient (yelling out of the waiting room): "Doctor! Help! I'm shrinking!"

Doctor (from inside his office): "I'm busy. You'll just have to be a little patient."

Patient: "I have a pain in my right knee."
Doctor: "What do you expect? It's an *87*-year-old knee."

Patient: "Yeah, but my other knee is 87 years old, too, and it doesn't hurt."

The doctor told his patient he would be back on his feet. He was right. The patient had to sell his car to pay his bill.

Woman to plastic surgeon: "Thanks for the lift!"

Q. What's the difference between an ICU nurse and a terrorist?

A. You can negotiate with a terrorist.

"OF COURSE, I'M THE ONLY PERSON YOU KNOW WITHOUT A CURE FOR YOUR COLD. I'M A DOCTOR."

Q. Why did the cannibal go to the psychiatrist?

A. He was fed up with people.

Q. What do you call a marriage between two doctors?

A. A paradox.

"**D**oc, I think my wife is going deaf."
"Try this: Stand a few feet away and ask a question. If she doesn't answer, move closer. Keep doing this until she answers to get an idea of how hard of hearing she is."

The man went home and walked in the door, calling out, "Honey, what's for dinner?" No answer. He moved closer and tried again. Still, no answer. He did this three times until he was right next to her.

"I said, 'Honey, what's for dinner?'"

"For the fourth time: Meatloaf!"

Q. How can a woman scare a gynecologist?

A. Become a ventriloquist.

Q. How many hospital CEOs does it take to wallpaper an average nurses' station?

A. Two, if you slice them thin enough.

Youth says, "I can't wait."
Old age says, "Wait, I can't."

"Doctor, when I press on my arm it hurts. When I press on my stomach, it hurts. When I press on my leg, it hurts. What's wrong with me?"

"You have a broken finger."

Patient: "You've got to help me. I have amnesia. What should I do?"

Doctor: "Go home and forget about it."

"I had the toughest time of my life. First I got angina pectoris, then atherosclerosis. As I was recovering from these, I got tuberculosis, pneumonia, and phlebitis. Then they gave me hypodermics. Appendicitis was followed by tonsillectomy. These gave way to aphasia and hypertrophic cirrhosis. I completely lost my memory with amnesia. I know I had diabetes and acute indigestion, besides gastritis, rheumatism, lumbago and neuritis. I don't know how I pulled through."

"But at least you did."

"I had to. I couldn't get the medical clerk job if I didn't pass the spelling test!"

Two little boys were discussing their hospital experiences. The older one asked, "Are you medical or surgical?"

The other little boy said, "I don't know. How can you tell?"

"Well," replied the more savvy of the two, "were you sick when you were admitted, or did they make you sick after you got here?"

Old Dr. Dillon still made house calls. One afternoon he was called to the Bixley house. Mrs. Bixley was in terrible pain.

The doctor came out of the bedroom a minute after he'd gone in and asked Mr. Bixley, "Do you have a hammer?"

A puzzled Mr. Bixley went to the garage and returned with a hammer. The doctor thanked him and went back into the bedroom.

A moment later, he came out and asked, "Do you have a chisel?" Mr. Bixley complied with the request.

In the next ten minutes, Dr. Dillon asked for and received a pair of pliers, a screwdriver and a hacksaw. The last request got to Mr. Bixley. He asked, "What are you doing to my wife?"

"Not a thing," replied old Doc Dillon. "I can't get my instrument bag open."

One doctor to another in hospital corridor, "I usually take two aspirins every four or five patients."

The doctor was trying to encourage a gloomy patient. "You're not in any real danger," he said. "Why, I've had the same thing myself."

"I see," moaned the dour faced man. "But did you have the same doctor?"

Patient to Nurse: "No, I don't feel listless. In fact, if I felt that good, I wouldn't even be here."

Patient: "Doctor, you've got to help me. Some mornings I wake up and think I'm Donald Duck. Other mornings I think I'm Mickey Mouse."

Doctor: "Hmmmm, and how long have you been having these disney spells?"

A woman went to a large medical clinic. She was seen by one of the new doctors, but after about four minutes in the exam room, she burst out, screaming as she ran down the hall. An older doctor stopped and asked her what was wrong, and after she explained, had her sit down and relax in another room.

The older doctor marched back to the first and demanded, "What's the matter with you? Mrs. Terry is 63 years old, she has four grown children and seven grandchildren, and you told her she was *pregnant?*"

The new doctor smiled smugly as he continued to write on his clipboard. "Cured her hiccups, though, didn't I?"

A Spoonful of Laughter Helps the Medicine Go Down

A DICTIONARY OF MEDICAL TERMS

Benign .... What you be after you be eight

Artery .... The study of paintings

Bacteria .... Back door to cafeteria

Barium .... What doctors do when patients die

Cesarean Section .... A neighborhood in Rome

Carcinoma .... A valley in California, notable for its heavy smog

CAT scan .... Searching for kitty

Cauterize .... Made eye contact with her

Colic .... A sheep dog

Coma .... A punctuation mark

D & C .... Where Washington is

Dilate .... To live long

Enema .... Not a friend

Fester .... Quicker than someone else

Fibula .... A small lie

Flatulence .... The emergency vehicle that picks you up after you get run over by a steam roller

Genital .... Non-Jewish person

G.I. Series .... World Series of military baseball

Hangnail .... What you hang your coat on

Impotent .... Distinguished, well known

Labor Pain .... Getting hurt at work

Lymph .... To walk with a lisp

Medical Staff .... A doctor's cane

Morbid .... A higher offer than I bid

Nitrates .... Cheaper than day rates

Node .... I knew it

Outpatient .... A person who has fainted

Pap Smear .... A fatherhood test

Pelvis .... Second cousin to Elvis

Post Operative .... A letter carrier

Recovery Room .... Place to do upholstery

Rectum .... Damn near killed him

Secretion .... Hiding something

Seizure .... Roman emperor

Tablet .... A small table

Terminal Illness .... Getting sick at the airport

Testicle .... A humorous question on an exam

Tumor .... More than one

Urine .... Opposite of you're out

Varicose .... Near by

SIGNS

Sign in hospital lab: "Be nice to bacteria. It's the only culture some people have."

Sign on the door of the maternity ward: "Push – Push – Push"

Sign in a podiatrist's window: "Time wounds all heels."

Optometrist's Office: "If you don't see what you're looking for, you've come to the right place."

Featured in a local restaurant: "Health Care Reform Stew: Don't ask what's in it— just swallow hard and pay the bill."

In a Florida maternity ward: "No children allowed."

In a health food shop window: "Closed due to illness."

QUOTES

" **T**here ain't much fun in medicine, but there's a lot of medicine in fun!"   *- Josh Billings*

" **T**he New England Journal of Medicine reports that nine out of 10 doctors agree that one out of 10 doctors is an idiot."   *- Jay Leno*

" **T**he medical profession is always looking for new things to stick as far as possible into our various bodily orifices. Those procedures are uncomfortable, but there's an important medical reason why doctors perform them: to win big cash prizes in the American Medical Association's competition to see who can insert an object the farthest into a patient."
- Dave Barry

" **I** said to my doctor, 'I've broken my arm in several places.' He said, 'Don't go to those places.'"
- Henny Youngman

" **B**ut wait ... perhaps we've been wrong to blindly follow the medical traditions and superstitions of the past century. Perhaps we should test those assumptions analytically through experimentation and the scientific method. Perhaps this scientific method could be extended to other fields such as natural science. Perhaps I could lead the way to an age of rebirth.................Naaaaaaaa!"
- Theodoric, Medieval Barber of York

"**B**lessed are the flexible, for they shall not be bent out of shape."   *- Dr. Michael McGriff*

TOP TEN SIGNS YOUR PATIENT IS REALLY A NURSE . . .

10. Records her own I&O (and also her roommate's).

9. Makes her own bed, complete with hospital corners.

8. Reads her own chart to make sure no one wrote "obese" in it.

7. Takes her own pulse while you take her temperature.

6. Asks if he is to be "NPO" tonight.

5. Strolls over to nurses' station to answer phones when she's bored.

4. Calls out suggestions to the code team when his roommate arrests.

3. Takes out her own IV or foley catheter.

2. Uses the telephone to call the nurses' station if no one answers her call light.

1. Has a tattoo on her chest that reads "NO CPR."

MEDICAL MYSTERIES...

Do Roman paramedics refer to IV's as "4's"?

According to a commercial, three out of five people suffer from hemorrhoids. Does that mean the other two enjoy them?

Why do the voices never say, "You're meds need adjusting"?

If someone with multiple personalities threatens suicide... is it considered a hostage situation?

Isn't it scary that doctors call what they do "practice"?

"THAT'S WHAT I LIKE ABOUT PETERSON, HE DOESN'T LET A LITTLE ILLNESS KEEP HIM OFF THE JOB."

DID YOU KNOW . . .

In 1845 Boston had an ordinance banning bathing unless you had a doctor's prescription.

Unless you have a doctor's note, it's illegal to buy ice cream after 6:00 P.M. in Newark, New Jersey.

CHARTING CHORTLES

The following statements were found on patients' charts from a variety of health care settings:

"The patient left the hospital feeling much better except for her original complaint."

"Patient has two teenage children, but no other abnormalities."

"Large brown stool ambulating in the hall."

"Patient was seen in consultation by Dr. Blank, who felt we should sit on the abdomen and I agree."

"The pelvic examination will be done later on the floor."

"Skin: somewhat pale but present."

"The lab test indicated abnormal lover function."

"Exam of genitalia reveals that he is circus sized."

"Both breasts are equal and reactive to light and accommodation."

"Rectal exam revealed a normal sized thyroid."

"Since she can't get pregnant with her husband, I thought that you might like to work her up."

"Patient had waffles for breakfast and anorexia for lunch."

"Patient's past medical history has been remarkably insignificant with only a 40-pound weight gain in the past three days."

"Patient has left his white blood cells at another hospital."

"The patient has no past history of suicides."

"Patient refused autopsy."

"Healthy appearing decrepit 69-year-old male, mentally alert but forgetful."

"Discharge status: alive, but without permission."

"The patient is tearful and crying constantly. She also appears to be depressed."

"Patient has chest pain if she lies on her left side for over a year."

"On the 2nd day the knee was better and on the 3rd day it completely disappeared."

"She has had no rigors or chills, but her husband states that she was very hot in bed last night."

"The patient has been depressed ever since she began seeing me in 1993."

"She stated that she had been constipated for most of her life until 1989 when she got a divorce."

"The patient was in his usual state of good health until his airplane ran out of gas and crashed."

"I saw your patient today, who is still under our car for physical therapy."

"The patient lives at home with his mother, father, and pet turtle, who is presently enrolled in day care three times a week."

"She is numb from her toes down."

"Exam of genitalia was completely negative except for the right foot."

"While in the emergency room, she was examined, X-rated and sent home."

"The patient was to have a bowel resection. However, he took a job as stockbroker instead."

"Coming from Detroit, this man has no children."

"When she fainted, her eyes rolled around the room."

"Examination reveals a well-developed male lying in bed with his family in no distress."

"Currently she is taking no films though anti-inflammatories and Naprosyn have given her some relief."

"Patient is short of breath even at the thought of exertion."

"The patient had a gunshot wound in the grocery store."

"The patient is functionally illetrate."

"The patient fell off a driveway onto a ladder."

"She lives in an environment that is not fit for human consumption."

"Although alert and generally oriented, she tends to suffer from good judgement."

"The mother has been doing a nice job of manipulating the foot with diaper changes."

"He has pain when he ambulates around his suture lines."

"The skin was pink to the touch."

"He was seeing people who were dead and suffering from shortness of breath."

"The patient is 76 years old . . . His mother is elderly also."

"He was in a ninety-degree room with only an osculating fan."

"The wound is pink, irregular and beginning to ambulate."

"The lungs are clear, except for the congestion."

"She hasn't had any gastrointestinal problems since her husband died eight years ago."

"She broke her hip when she slipped and fell on a wet floor. She is practically blind and didn't notice the floor."

"The baby was delivered, the cord clamped and cut and handed to the pediatrician, who breathed and cried immediately."

"The skin was moist and dry."

"Between you and me, we ought to be able to get this lady pregnant."

"Occasional, constant, infrequent headaches."

"Patient was alert and unresponsive."

"Patient deserves a colonoscopy."

A new patient at the clinic just finished filling out his health history form. The nurse noticed that under "sex" he checked both "M" and "F" and added, "and if I'm feeling strong enough, sometimes on Wed., too."

A patient was severely nauseated. His doctor, who was making rounds, was summoned. The nurse's notes that day said, "Mr. Smith was nauseated and Dr. Martin came up."

Dictated: "Patient had a Pap smear today."
Transcribed: "Patient had a Pabst Beer today."

THE HMO HYMN
(Sung to the tune of "Old One Hundredth")
From JNJ by Brenda W. Quinn, BA

Praise God from Whom all blessings flow
That He has moved the HMO.
To reconsider why they pay
After a time of long delay.

Let all that dwell below the skies
Cry out "Unfair!" as we arise.
We never make a payment late,
And yet we must negotiate.

The doctor that we long to see
Has got no time for you and me.
And time with patients he must shirk
To do the endless paperwork.

When Jesus in a manger lay,
So long ago, so far away,
Twas in a stable, don't you know,
Cause Mary had an HMO.

Praise God from whom all blessings flow.
And keep us healthy here below.
Send down Your blessings double quick.
We can't afford, Lord, to be sick!

NURSE-Y RHYMES

From JNJ by Elaine Tuten RN

Hickory, Dickory, Doc.
The nurse works 'round the clock.
Her shift is done, but home she runs
To dust and cook and mop!

Hey diddle, diddle,
There's no time to fiddle!
The nurse runs from room to room.
The doctors say, "STAT!"
You do this and do that
And the next shift can't get here too soon!

Little nurse Sue,
Come pass your pills.
The patients are ailing
With aches, pains and ills.
And, "Where is the nurse with my PRN?"
She's running a code in Room 2110!

Doctor Spratt said, "Do this STAT!"
The nurse thought, "In your dreams!
I've meds to pass and rounds to make
And admits not yet seen!"

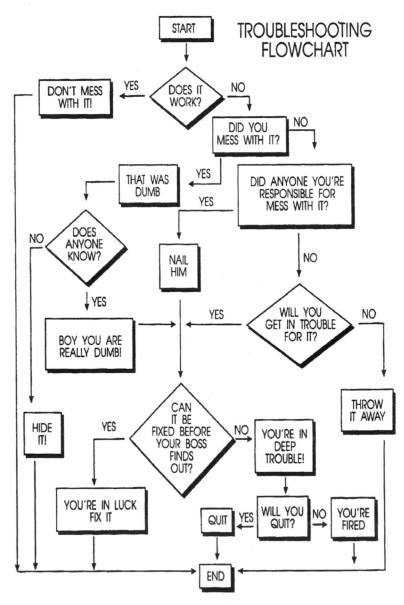

Permission to reprint: Journal of Nursing Jocularity